Unpack Your Heart

Journal

RITA CARTER

Unpack Your Heart Journal

HOV Publishing is a division of HOV, LLC.
www.hovpub.com
email: hopeofvision@gmail.com

Front Cover Design and Inside layout by HOV Design Solutions
A Hope of Vision Journal Collection

To learn more about Rita's coaching and speaking services or to schedule a free discovery call, email Rita Carter at Clientcare@breakthroughready.com.

Visit www.breakthroughready.com for your free relationship checklist and to sign-up for our Monday Motivation newsletter.

Social Media:
Facebook: https://www.facebook.com/BreakthroughwithRita
Instagram: https://www.instagram.com/breakthroughwithrita/
LinkedIn: linkedin.com/in/rita-carter

ISBN Paperback: 978-1-955107-30-3
ISBN PB Journal: 978-1-955107-29-7
ISBN eBook: 978-1-955107-28-0

Printed in the United States of America

The journal component of Unpack Your Heart: 7 Steps to Rewriting Your Love Story by Rita Carter is designed to offer readers a flexible and personalized space to record your thoughts, reflections, and insights as you navigate the seven-step process. This unstructured journal section encourages creativity, free expression, and deeper introspection, allowing readers to fully engage with their journey toward rewriting your love story.

Unpack Your Heart

Journal

KEY FEATURES:
DO SOMETHING DIFFERENT

1. Willingness and Prayer

- **Question:** What areas of my life do I need to surrender to God more fully?

- **Action:** Set aside a specific time each day for prayer, focusing on asking God for willingness to change and for His guidance.

- **Journal Prompt:** Reflect on a time when you resisted God's will. How did that affect your life? How can you cultivate a heart of willingness today?

2. Accountability and Communication

- **Question:** Who in my life can I trust to hold me accountable and support my growth?

  ____
  ____
  ____
  ____
  ____
  ____

- **Action:** Identify and reach out to an accountability partner. Share your goals and ask for their support and honesty.

  ____
  ____
  ____
  ____
  ____
  ____

- **Journal Prompt:** Write about a recent conversation where you felt truly heard and understood. What made it effective? How can you replicate this in other relationships?

  ____
  ____
  ____
  ____
  ____
  ____

3. Forgiveness

- **Question:** Who do I need to forgive, and who might need my forgiveness?

- **Action:** Write a letter of forgiveness (whether you send it or not) to someone who has hurt you, or seek forgiveness from someone you have wronged.

- **Journal Prompt:** Reflect on how holding onto grudges has affected your well-being. How does choosing to forgive change your perspective?

4. Trust, Intimacy and Vulnerability

- **Question:** What fears are preventing me from fully trusting God and others?

  ____
  ____
  ____
  ____
  ____
  ____

- **Action:** Take a step of faith in a situation where you have been hesitant. Trust in God's provision and the support of those around you.

  ____
  ____
  ____
  ____
  ____
  ____

- **Journal Prompt:** Describe a time when you took a leap of faith. What was the outcome? How can you build on that experience to trust more fully now?

  ____
  ____
  ____
  ____
  ____
  ____

- **Question:** What barriers do I have to being fully open and vulnerable with loved ones?

____
____
____
____
____
____

- **Action:** Share a personal story or a deep feeling with someone you trust, allowing yourself to be vulnerable.

____
____
____
____
____
____

- **Journal Prompt:** Reflect on a moment when someone was vulnerable with you. How did it impact your relationship? How can vulnerability enhance your connections?

____
____
____
____
____
____

5. **Building on a Solid Foundation**

- **Question:** What foundational truths and values do I need to reaffirm in my life?

- **Action:** Create a personal mission statement or a list of core values based on biblical principles. Review and meditate on it daily.

- **Journal Prompt:** Think about a time when you felt grounded and secure in your faith. What practices helped you build that foundation? How can you reinforce them now?

6. Setting Boundaries

- **Question:** Where do I need to set healthier boundaries in my relationships?

- **Action:** Identify one relationship where boundaries are lacking or unclear. Have a conversation to establish or reaffirm these boundaries.

- **Journal Prompt:** Reflect on a relationship where setting boundaries improved the dynamic. How did it change, and what did you learn from the experience?

7. Rediscover and Adventure

- **Question:** What passions or interests have I neglected that I can rediscover?

- **Action:** Plan an activity or an adventure that reignites an old passion or explores a new interest. Document your experience and what you learned about yourself.

- **Journal Prompt:** Write about a time when you stepped out of your comfort zone and tried something new. What did you discover about yourself? How can you continue to embrace new experiences?

Unpack Your Heart

Journal

SCRIPTURE GUIDE

These scriptures can be used as a journal guide to deepen your reflection and growth through each step.

1. Willingness and Prayer

- **Matthew 26:39** - "Going a little farther, he fell with his face to the ground and prayed, 'My Father, if it is possible, may this cup be taken from me. Yet not as I will, but as you will.'"
- **Philippians 4:6-7** - "Do not be anxious about anything, but in every situation, by prayer and petition, with thanksgiving, present your requests to God. And the peace of God, which transcends all understanding, will guard your hearts and your minds in Christ Jesus."
- **James 1:5** - "If any of you lacks wisdom, you should ask God, who gives generously to all without finding fault, and it will be given to you."

2. Accountability and Communication

- **Proverbs 27:17** - "As iron sharpens iron, so one person sharpens another."
- **James 5:16** - "Therefore confess your sins to each other and pray for each other so that you may be healed. The prayer of a righteous person is powerful and effective."
- **Ephesians 4:15** - "Instead, speaking the truth in love, we will grow to become in every respect the mature body of him who is the head, that is, Christ."

3. Forgiveness

- **Ephesians 4:32** - "Be kind and compassionate to one another, forgiving each other, just as in Christ God forgave you."
- **Colossians 3:13** - "Bear with each other and forgive one another if any of you has a grievance against someone. Forgive as the Lord forgave you."
- **Matthew 6:14-15** - "For if you forgive other people when they sin against you, your heavenly Father will also forgive you. But if you do not forgive others their sins, your Father will not forgive your sins."

4. Trust, Intimacy and Vulnerability

- **Proverbs 3:5-6** - "Trust in the Lord with all your heart and lean not on your own understanding; in all your ways submit to him, and he will make your paths straight."
- **Psalm 37:3-5** - "Trust in the Lord and do good; dwell in the land and enjoy safe pasture. Take delight in the Lord, and he will give you the desires of your heart. Commit your way to the Lord; trust in him and he will do this."
- **Jeremiah 17:7-8** - "But blessed is the one who trusts in the Lord, whose confidence is in him. They will be like a tree planted by the water that sends out its roots by the stream."

- **1 Corinthians 13:4-7** - "Love is patient, love is kind. It does not envy, it does not boast, it is not proud. It does not dishonor others, it is not self-seeking, it is not easily angered, it keeps no record of wrongs. Love does not delight in evil but rejoices with the truth. It always protects, always trusts, always hopes, always perseveres."
- **Genesis 2:24-25** - "That is why a man leaves his father and mother and is united to his wife, and they become one flesh. Adam and his wife were both naked, and they felt no shame."
- **1 John 4:18** - "There is no fear in love. But perfect love drives out fear, because fear has to do with punishment. The one who fears is not made perfect in love."

5. Building on a Solid Foundation

- **Matthew 7:24-25** - "Therefore everyone who hears these words of mine and puts them into practice is like a wise man who built his house on the rock. The rain came down, the streams rose, and the winds blew and beat against that house; yet it did not fall, because it had its foundation on the rock."
- **1 Corinthians 3:11** - "For no one can lay any foundation other than the one already laid, which is Jesus Christ."
- **Ephesians 2:19-22** - "Consequently, you are no longer foreigners and strangers, but fellow citizens

with God's people and also members of his household, built on the foundation of the apostles and prophets, with Christ Jesus himself as the chief cornerstone. In him the whole building is joined together and rises to become a holy temple in the Lord."

6. Setting Boundaries

- **Proverbs 4:23** - "Above all else, guard your heart, for everything you do flows from it."
- **Galatians 6:2-5** - "Carry each other's burdens, and in this way you will fulfill the law of Christ. If anyone thinks they are something when they are not, they deceive themselves. Each one should test their own actions. Then they can take pride in themselves alone, without comparing themselves to someone else, for each one should carry their own load."
- **2 Corinthians 6:14** - "Do not be yoked together with unbelievers. For what do righteousness and wickedness have in common? Or what fellowship can light have with darkness?"

7. Rediscover and Adventure

- **Isaiah 43:18-19** - "Forget the former things; do not dwell on the past. See, I am doing a new thing! Now it springs up; do you not perceive it? I am making a way in the wilderness and streams in the wasteland."

- **2 Corinthians 5:17** - "Therefore, if anyone is in Christ, the new creation has come: The old has gone, the new is here!"
- **Psalm 32:8** - "I will instruct you and teach you in the way you should go; I will counsel you with my loving eye on you."

These scriptures can serve as a powerful journal guide, providing wisdom, encouragement, and insight as you work through each step of rewriting your love story.

Unpack Your Heart

Journal

SUBJECT: ______________________ DATE: / /

Sunday Monday Tuesday Wednesday Thursday Friday Saturday

SUBJECT: ______________________ DATE: / /

Sunday Monday Tuesday Wednesday Thursday Friday Saturday

SUBJECT: ______________________ DATE: / /

Sunday Monday Tuesday Wednesday Thursday Friday Saturday

SUBJECT: ______________________ DATE: / /

Sunday Monday Tuesday Wednesday Thursday Friday Saturday

SUBJECT: ______________________ DATE: / /

Sunday Monday Tuesday Wednesday Thursday Friday Saturday

SUBJECT: ________________________ DATE: / /

Sunday Monday Tuesday Wednesday Thursday Friday Saturday

SUBJECT: ______________________ DATE: / /

Sunday Monday Tuesday Wednesday Thursday Friday Saturday

SUBJECT: ______________________ DATE: / /

Sunday Monday Tuesday Wednesday Thursday Friday Saturday

SUBJECT: ______________________ DATE: / /

Sunday Monday Tuesday Wednesday Thursday Friday Saturday

SUBJECT: ______________________ DATE: / /

Sunday Monday Tuesday Wednesday Thursday Friday Saturday

SUBJECT: ______________________ DATE: / /

Sunday Monday Tuesday Wednesday Thursday Friday Saturday

SUBJECT: ____________________ DATE: / /

Sunday Monday Tuesday Wednesday Thursday Friday Saturday

SUBJECT: ______________________________ DATE: / /

Sunday Monday Tuesday Wednesday Thursday Friday Saturday

SUBJECT: ______________________ DATE: / /

Sunday Monday Tuesday Wednesday Thursday Friday Saturday

SUBJECT: ______________________ DATE: / /

Sunday Monday Tuesday Wednesday Thursday Friday Saturday

SUBJECT: ______________________ DATE: / /

Sunday Monday Tuesday Wednesday Thursday Friday Saturday

SUBJECT: ______________________ DATE: / /

Sunday Monday Tuesday Wednesday Thursday Friday Saturday

SUBJECT: ______________________ DATE: / /

Sunday Monday Tuesday Wednesday Thursday Friday Saturday

SUBJECT: ______________________ DATE: / /

Sunday Monday Tuesday Wednesday Thursday Friday Saturday

SUBJECT: ______________________ DATE: / /

Sunday Monday Tuesday Wednesday Thursday Friday Saturday

SUBJECT: ______________________ DATE: / /

Sunday Monday Tuesday Wednesday Thursday Friday Saturday

SUBJECT: ______________________ DATE: / /

Sunday Monday Tuesday Wednesday Thursday Friday Saturday

SUBJECT: ______________________ DATE: / /

Sunday Monday Tuesday Wednesday Thursday Friday Saturday

SUBJECT: ______________________ DATE: / /

Sunday Monday Tuesday Wednesday Thursday Friday Saturday

SUBJECT: ______________________ DATE: / /

Sunday Monday Tuesday Wednesday Thursday Friday Saturday

SUBJECT: ______________________ DATE: / /

Sunday Monday Tuesday Wednesday Thursday Friday Saturday

SUBJECT: ______________________ DATE: / /

Sunday Monday Tuesday Wednesday Thursday Friday Saturday

SUBJECT: ______________________ DATE: / /

Sunday Monday Tuesday Wednesday Thursday Friday Saturday

SUBJECT: ______________________ DATE: / /

Sunday Monday Tuesday Wednesday Thursday Friday Saturday

SUBJECT: ______________________ DATE: / /

Sunday Monday Tuesday Wednesday Thursday Friday Saturday

SUBJECT: ______________________ DATE: / /

Sunday Monday Tuesday Wednesday Thursday Friday Saturday

SUBJECT: ______________________ DATE: / /

Sunday Monday Tuesday Wednesday Thursday Friday Saturday

SUBJECT: ________________________ DATE: / /

Sunday Monday Tuesday Wednesday Thursday Friday Saturday

SUBJECT: ______________________ DATE: / /

Sunday Monday Tuesday Wednesday Thursday Friday Saturday

SUBJECT: ____________________ DATE: / /

Sunday Monday Tuesday Wednesday Thursday Friday Saturday

SUBJECT: ____________________ DATE: / /

Sunday Monday Tuesday Wednesday Thursday Friday Saturday

SUBJECT: ______________________ DATE: / /

Sunday Monday Tuesday Wednesday Thursday Friday Saturday

SUBJECT: ______________________ DATE: / /

Sunday Monday Tuesday Wednesday Thursday Friday Saturday

SUBJECT: ______________________ DATE: / /

Sunday Monday Tuesday Wednesday Thursday Friday Saturday

SUBJECT: ______________________ DATE: / /

Sunday Monday Tuesday Wednesday Thursday Friday Saturday

SUBJECT: ______________________________ DATE: / /

Sunday Monday Tuesday Wednesday Thursday Friday Saturday

SUBJECT: ______________________ DATE: / /

Sunday Monday Tuesday Wednesday Thursday Friday Saturday

SUBJECT: ______________________ DATE: / /

Sunday Monday Tuesday Wednesday Thursday Friday Saturday

SUBJECT: ______________________ DATE: / /

Sunday Monday Tuesday Wednesday Thursday Friday Saturday

SUBJECT: ______________________ DATE: / /

Sunday Monday Tuesday Wednesday Thursday Friday Saturday

SUBJECT: ________________________ DATE: / /

Sunday Monday Tuesday Wednesday Thursday Friday Saturday

SUBJECT: ______________________ DATE: / /

Sunday Monday Tuesday Wednesday Thursday Friday Saturday

SUBJECT: ______________________ DATE: / /

Sunday Monday Tuesday Wednesday Thursday Friday Saturday

SUBJECT: ______________________ DATE: / /

Sunday Monday Tuesday Wednesday Thursday Friday Saturday

SUBJECT: ____________________ DATE: / /

Sunday Monday Tuesday Wednesday Thursday Friday Saturday

SUBJECT: ______________________ DATE: / /

Sunday Monday Tuesday Wednesday Thursday Friday Saturday

SUBJECT: ______________________ DATE: / /

Sunday Monday Tuesday Wednesday Thursday Friday Saturday

SUBJECT: ____________________ DATE: / /

Sunday Monday Tuesday Wednesday Thursday Friday Saturday

SUBJECT: ____________________ DATE: / /

Sunday Monday Tuesday Wednesday Thursday Friday Saturday

SUBJECT: ______________________ DATE: / /

Sunday Monday Tuesday Wednesday Thursday Friday Saturday

SUBJECT: ____________________ DATE: / /

Sunday Monday Tuesday Wednesday Thursday Friday Saturday

SUBJECT: ______________________ DATE: / /

Sunday Monday Tuesday Wednesday Thursday Friday Saturday

SUBJECT: ______________________ DATE: / /

Sunday Monday Tuesday Wednesday Thursday Friday Saturday

SUBJECT: ______________________ DATE: / /

Sunday Monday Tuesday Wednesday Thursday Friday Saturday

SUBJECT: ______________________ DATE: / /

Sunday Monday Tuesday Wednesday Thursday Friday Saturday

SUBJECT: ______________________ DATE: / /

Sunday Monday Tuesday Wednesday Thursday Friday Saturday

SUBJECT: ______________________ DATE: / /

Sunday Monday Tuesday Wednesday Thursday Friday Saturday

SUBJECT: ______________________ DATE: / /

Sunday Monday Tuesday Wednesday Thursday Friday Saturday

SUBJECT: ______________________ DATE: / /

Sunday Monday Tuesday Wednesday Thursday Friday Saturday

SUBJECT: ______________________ DATE: / /

Sunday Monday Tuesday Wednesday Thursday Friday Saturday

SUBJECT: ______________________________ DATE: / /

Sunday Monday Tuesday Wednesday Thursday Friday Saturday

SUBJECT: ______________________ DATE: / /

Sunday Monday Tuesday Wednesday Thursday Friday Saturday

SUBJECT: ______________________ DATE: / /

Sunday Monday Tuesday Wednesday Thursday Friday Saturday

SUBJECT: ______________________ DATE: / /

Sunday Monday Tuesday Wednesday Thursday Friday Saturday

SUBJECT: ______________________ DATE: / /

Sunday Monday Tuesday Wednesday Thursday Friday Saturday

SUBJECT: ______________________ DATE: / /

Sunday Monday Tuesday Wednesday Thursday Friday Saturday

SUBJECT: ______________________ DATE: / /

Sunday Monday Tuesday Wednesday Thursday Friday Saturday

SUBJECT: ______________________ DATE: / /

Sunday Monday Tuesday Wednesday Thursday Friday Saturday

SUBJECT: ______________________ DATE: / /

Sunday Monday Tuesday Wednesday Thursday Friday Saturday

SUBJECT: ______________________ DATE: / /

Sunday Monday Tuesday Wednesday Thursday Friday Saturday

SUBJECT: ______________________ DATE: / /

Sunday Monday Tuesday Wednesday Thursday Friday Saturday

SUBJECT: ______________________ DATE: / /

Sunday Monday Tuesday Wednesday Thursday Friday Saturday

SUBJECT: ______________________ DATE: / /

Sunday Monday Tuesday Wednesday Thursday Friday Saturday

SUBJECT: ______________________ DATE: / /

Sunday Monday Tuesday Wednesday Thursday Friday Saturday

SUBJECT: ______________________ DATE: / /

Sunday Monday Tuesday Wednesday Thursday Friday Saturday

SUBJECT: ______________________ DATE: / /

Sunday Monday Tuesday Wednesday Thursday Friday Saturday

SUBJECT: ______________________ DATE: / /

Sunday Monday Tuesday Wednesday Thursday Friday Saturday

SUBJECT: ______________________ DATE: / /

Sunday Monday Tuesday Wednesday Thursday Friday Saturday

SUBJECT: ______________________ DATE: / /

Sunday Monday Tuesday Wednesday Thursday Friday Saturday

SUBJECT: ______________________ DATE: / /

Sunday Monday Tuesday Wednesday Thursday Friday Saturday

SUBJECT: ____________________ DATE: / /

Sunday Monday Tuesday Wednesday Thursday Friday Saturday

SUBJECT: ______________________ DATE: / /

Sunday Monday Tuesday Wednesday Thursday Friday Saturday

SUBJECT: ______________________ DATE: / /

Sunday Monday Tuesday Wednesday Thursday Friday Saturday

SUBJECT: ____________________ DATE: / /

Sunday Monday Tuesday Wednesday Thursday Friday Saturday

SUBJECT: ______________________ DATE: / /

Sunday Monday Tuesday Wednesday Thursday Friday Saturday

SUBJECT: ______________________________ DATE: / /

Sunday Monday Tuesday Wednesday Thursday Friday Saturday

SUBJECT: ______________________ DATE: / /

Sunday Monday Tuesday Wednesday Thursday Friday Saturday

SUBJECT: ______________________ DATE: / /

Sunday Monday Tuesday Wednesday Thursday Friday Saturday

SUBJECT: ______________________ DATE: / /

Sunday Monday Tuesday Wednesday Thursday Friday Saturday

SUBJECT: ______________________ DATE: / /

Sunday Monday Tuesday Wednesday Thursday Friday Saturday

SUBJECT: ______________________ DATE: / /

Sunday Monday Tuesday Wednesday Thursday Friday Saturday

SUBJECT: ______________________ DATE: / /

Sunday Monday Tuesday Wednesday Thursday Friday Saturday

SUBJECT: ______________________ DATE: / /

Sunday Monday Tuesday Wednesday Thursday Friday Saturday

SUBJECT: ______________________ DATE: / /

Sunday Monday Tuesday Wednesday Thursday Friday Saturday

SUBJECT: ____________________ DATE: / /

Sunday Monday Tuesday Wednesday Thursday Friday Saturday

SUBJECT: ______________________ DATE: / /

Sunday Monday Tuesday Wednesday Thursday Friday Saturday

SUBJECT: ______________________ DATE: / /

Sunday Monday Tuesday Wednesday Thursday Friday Saturday

SUBJECT: ______________________ DATE: / /

Sunday Monday Tuesday Wednesday Thursday Friday Saturday

SUBJECT: ______________________ DATE: / /

Sunday Monday Tuesday Wednesday Thursday Friday Saturday

SUBJECT: ______________________ DATE: / /

Sunday Monday Tuesday Wednesday Thursday Friday Saturday

SUBJECT: ______________________ DATE: / /

Sunday Monday Tuesday Wednesday Thursday Friday Saturday

SUBJECT: ______________________________ DATE: / /

Sunday Monday Tuesday Wednesday Thursday Friday Saturday

SUBJECT: ______________________ DATE: / /

Sunday Monday Tuesday Wednesday Thursday Friday Saturday

SUBJECT: ______________________ DATE: / /

Sunday Monday Tuesday Wednesday Thursday Friday Saturday

SUBJECT: ____________________ DATE: / /

Sunday Monday Tuesday Wednesday Thursday Friday Saturday

SUBJECT: ______________________ DATE: / /

Sunday Monday Tuesday Wednesday Thursday Friday Saturday

SUBJECT: ______________________ DATE: / /

Sunday Monday Tuesday Wednesday Thursday Friday Saturday

SUBJECT: ______________________ DATE: / /

Sunday Monday Tuesday Wednesday Thursday Friday Saturday

SUBJECT: ______________________ DATE: / /

Sunday Monday Tuesday Wednesday Thursday Friday Saturday

SUBJECT: ______________________ DATE: / /

Sunday Monday Tuesday Wednesday Thursday Friday Saturday

SUBJECT: ______________________ DATE: / /

Sunday Monday Tuesday Wednesday Thursday Friday Saturday

SUBJECT: ________________________ DATE: / /

Sunday Monday Tuesday Wednesday Thursday Friday Saturday

SUBJECT: ______________________ DATE: / /

Sunday Monday Tuesday Wednesday Thursday Friday Saturday

SUBJECT: ______________________ DATE: / /

Sunday Monday Tuesday Wednesday Thursday Friday Saturday

SUBJECT: ______________________ DATE: / /

Sunday Monday Tuesday Wednesday Thursday Friday Saturday

SUBJECT: ______________________ DATE: / /

Sunday Monday Tuesday Wednesday Thursday Friday Saturday

SUBJECT: ______________________ DATE: / /

Sunday Monday Tuesday Wednesday Thursday Friday Saturday

SUBJECT: ____________________________ DATE: / /

Sunday Monday Tuesday Wednesday Thursday Friday Saturday

SUBJECT: ______________________ DATE: / /

Sunday Monday Tuesday Wednesday Thursday Friday Saturday

SUBJECT: ______________________ DATE: / /

Sunday Monday Tuesday Wednesday Thursday Friday Saturday

SUBJECT: ______________________ DATE: / /

Sunday Monday Tuesday Wednesday Thursday Friday Saturday

SUBJECT: ______________________ DATE: / /

Sunday Monday Tuesday Wednesday Thursday Friday Saturday

SUBJECT: ______________________ DATE: / /

Sunday Monday Tuesday Wednesday Thursday Friday Saturday

SUBJECT: ____________________ DATE: / /

Sunday Monday Tuesday Wednesday Thursday Friday Saturday

SUBJECT: ______________________ DATE: / /

Sunday Monday Tuesday Wednesday Thursday Friday Saturday

SUBJECT: ______________________ DATE: / /

Sunday Monday Tuesday Wednesday Thursday Friday Saturday

SUBJECT: ______________________ DATE: / /

Sunday Monday Tuesday Wednesday Thursday Friday Saturday

SUBJECT: ______________________ DATE: / /

Sunday Monday Tuesday Wednesday Thursday Friday Saturday

SUBJECT: ____________________ DATE: / /

Sunday Monday Tuesday Wednesday Thursday Friday Saturday

SUBJECT: ______________________ DATE: / /

Sunday Monday Tuesday Wednesday Thursday Friday Saturday

SUBJECT: ______________________ DATE: / /

Sunday Monday Tuesday Wednesday Thursday Friday Saturday

SUBJECT: ______________________ DATE: / /

Sunday Monday Tuesday Wednesday Thursday Friday Saturday

SUBJECT: ______________________ DATE: / /

Sunday Monday Tuesday Wednesday Thursday Friday Saturday

SUBJECT: ______________________ DATE: / /

Sunday Monday Tuesday Wednesday Thursday Friday Saturday

SUBJECT: ______________________ DATE: / /

Sunday Monday Tuesday Wednesday Thursday Friday Saturday

SUBJECT: ______________________ DATE: / /

Sunday Monday Tuesday Wednesday Thursday Friday Saturday

SUBJECT: ______________________ DATE: / /

Sunday Monday Tuesday Wednesday Thursday Friday Saturday

SUBJECT: ____________________ DATE: / /

Sunday Monday Tuesday Wednesday Thursday Friday Saturday

SUBJECT: ______________________ DATE: / /

Sunday Monday Tuesday Wednesday Thursday Friday Saturday

SUBJECT: ____________________ DATE: / /

Sunday Monday Tuesday Wednesday Thursday Friday Saturday

SUBJECT: ____________________ DATE: / /

Sunday Monday Tuesday Wednesday Thursday Friday Saturday

SUBJECT: ______________________ DATE: / /

Sunday Monday Tuesday Wednesday Thursday Friday Saturday

SUBJECT: ______________________ DATE: / /

Sunday Monday Tuesday Wednesday Thursday Friday Saturday

SUBJECT: ______________________ DATE: / /

Sunday Monday Tuesday Wednesday Thursday Friday Saturday

SUBJECT: ______________________ DATE: / /

Sunday Monday Tuesday Wednesday Thursday Friday Saturday

SUBJECT: ______________________ DATE: / /

Sunday Monday Tuesday Wednesday Thursday Friday Saturday

SUBJECT: ______________________ DATE: / /

Sunday Monday Tuesday Wednesday Thursday Friday Saturday

SUBJECT: ______________________ DATE: / /

Sunday Monday Tuesday Wednesday Thursday Friday Saturday

SUBJECT: ______________________ DATE: / /

Sunday Monday Tuesday Wednesday Thursday Friday Saturday

SUBJECT: ______________________ DATE: / /

Sunday Monday Tuesday Wednesday Thursday Friday Saturday

SUBJECT: ______________________ DATE: / /

Sunday Monday Tuesday Wednesday Thursday Friday Saturday

SUBJECT: ______________________ DATE: / /

Sunday Monday Tuesday Wednesday Thursday Friday Saturday

SUBJECT: ______________________ DATE: / /

Sunday Monday Tuesday Wednesday Thursday Friday Saturday

SUBJECT: ______________________ DATE: / /

Sunday Monday Tuesday Wednesday Thursday Friday Saturday

SUBJECT: ______________________ DATE: / /

Sunday Monday Tuesday Wednesday Thursday Friday Saturday

www.ingramcontent.com/pod-product-compliance
Lightning Source LLC
Chambersburg PA
CBHW040531170726
48295CB00012B/428
9781955107297